MESSENGERS FROM THE COSMOS

THE INFLUENCE OF CONTACTISM

ON HISTORY AND HUMANITY

© Giuseppe Corcione & Giovanni Pellegrino – 2024

Daniele Cataldi Publisher

Finished writing on November 1, 2024

Published on November 5, 2024

SUMMARY

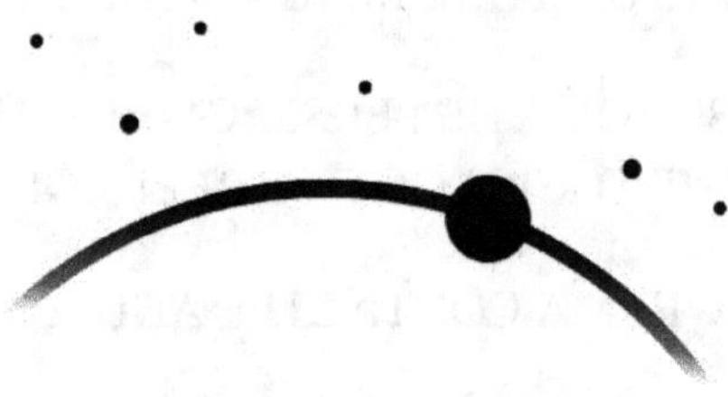

PREFACE

Not believing in UFOs and the existence of other living beings is a mistake. Their existence is not only supported by about a million testimonies, including those of many atheist scientists, but it is also confirmed by certain passages of Sacred Scripture, which, in some instances, clearly indicate the presence of extraterrestrials.

(Corrado Balducci, theologian)

First of all, we must understand what "contactism" means. We could say right away that it is a phenomenon involving those who claim to be in contact with alien intelligences. Modern contactism, which began to emerge around the 1950s worldwide, is characterized by a series of contacts and testimonies never experienced or collected in previous centuries. These weave a clear thread of the phenomenon, helping us understand the ongoing, though long-standing, official alien disclosure. Generally, contactees have never enjoyed a good reputation within social and ufological communities.

In this book, written by Pellegrino and Corcione, we will explore who these communicators were and how this dynamic unfolded in cultural contexts from the 1950s to today. The "Amicizia Case," which is still widely discussed today, falls within the realm of pure contactism. Italy, 1956: a group of Italian citizens (who did not know each other) was contacted, mainly through telepathy, by some extraterrestrials. Notable figures include Bruno Sammaciccia, Bruno Ghibaudi, Gaspare De Lama, Paolo Di Girolamo, and others.

The name "Amicizia" ("Friendship") came from the fact that these relationships were positive, with the extraterrestrials intending to help humanity. The extraterrestrials, or "aliens," were code-named W56, standing for "Viva 56" (the year of the first contacts), while other extraterrestrials, less favorably inclined toward humanity, were called CTR, short for "contrari" ("contrary").

During the last online meeting organized by the CUN group in Rome in March 2021, Gaspare De Lama, now nearly a centenarian, and his wife Mirella joined the session and shared their experiences with remarkable lucidity. At a certain point, the group split, and the experience ended.

De Lama recalled one of his last telepathic conversations with one of the stellar friends, who said to him: "Gasparone" (it seems he called him that affectionately), "do not be disheartened by the end of this experience; our mission has been successfully completed. We needed to connect with you to channel things in a certain way and introduce positivity that could counteract opposing and dangerous tendencies for humanity's fate. (It's worth noting this occurred amid the Cold War, international crises, and tensions. Similar contact groups were forming in other parts of the world.) So, do not be saddened; everything has gone well."

Through careful study, the conclusion reached is that this phenomenon has always existed and continues to exist today. They are likely civilizations vastly different from ours, capable of somehow entering and exiting this reality, shifting dimensions, unlike those who contacted or described them.

In a letter to Schrödinger dated 1935, Einstein wrote: "The real difficulty lies in the fact that physics is a kind of metaphysics; physics describes 'reality.' But we do not know what 'reality' is except through the physical description we provide." Therefore, we should expect anything. After all, we know well that our senses are merely impulses at a cerebral level. In the end, I believe that we unconsciously create what we call "Reality" under the aegis of creator Archetypes, which, due to our lack of understanding of their interactions with us, we call Aliens.

Let us conclude with a quote from Margherita Hack: "In our galaxy, there are one hundred billion stars, and in the universe, there are more than one hundred billion galaxies. Thinking we are unique is highly improbable."

The conclusions are yours to draw.

Ermelinda Calabria

PRESENTATION

In this book, we focus on contactees, who are the cornerstone of religious ufology, as they are often regarded as the new prophets of the space age, with some of them even founding new ufological religions.

It is important to note that religious interpretations of UFOs were present from the very beginning.

One of the first to assert that UFOs were spacecraft was the highly controversial George Adamski, the pioneer and most famous of the early contactees in the nascent field of ufology.

Going beyond the viewpoints of ufologists, Adamski and his fellow contactees added a spiritual and ethical dimension to the mystery of UFOs.

In 1952, Adamski claimed to have had personal contact with the occupants of alien spacecraft and was thus able to describe who they were, what they wanted, and what humanity could learn from them.

As a highly evolved race, far beyond ordinary human capabilities, these "space brothers" came to encourage the people of Earth to fulfill their spiritual destiny and take their place in cosmic consciousness.

From the outset, Adamski's words and those of other contactees reflected a distinctly soteriological and millenarian vision.

The UFO phenomenon expanded, revealing itself within a novel and authentically religious framework, so much so that the first ufological religions emerged.

Non-religious ufological organizations operated within the theoretical and methodological bounds of ordinary logic, yet they never seemed to come close to solving the UFO mystery.

In contrast, religious interpretations, such as those offered by some contactees, did not face the same limitations.

As religious narratives, they were able to place flying saucers within a mythological-religious context that was far more flexible and could be approached more directly according to the needs of understanding.

While non-religious ufological organizations sought tangible, indisputable evidence of UFO existence, followers of the contactees were content with compelling narratives.

In other words, they placed flying saucers within mythological-religious categories, a strategy often seen as superior to that of non-religious ufological organizations.

But what are the basic components of the contactees' stories?

First, the aliens reveal their presence to the contactees without the latter having any prior expectation.

Typically, contactees describe receiving a kind of telepathic message or intuition prompting them to visit an isolated location.

It is near this location that a flying saucer is said to land.

Contactees describe the beings aboard UFOs as humanoid but not ordinary.

On the contrary, they are described as exceptionally beautiful in appearance and extraordinary in intellect.

The aliens are typically fair-skinned or blonde, tall, and often have shoulder-length hair.

Moreover, they usually wear jumpsuits, though other types of clothing have also been described.

For instance, Adamski spoke of beautiful attire and hairstyles among the women of Venus.

According to contactees, the occupants of UFOs may come from planets within our solar system or from planets orbiting more distant stars.

At the heart of the contactees' accounts is the belief that human-like beings live in various parts of the universe.

However, the spiritual and technological development of these aliens is vastly different from ours.

The people of Earth are considered primitive compared to the aliens visiting our planet.

They preach a message based on love, peace, and responsibility and firmly urge Earth's inhabitants to strive for spiritual growth.

It is not uncommon for these aliens to represent interplanetary associations, with the contactees tasked with preparing Earth's people to join these universal associations.

Before this can happen, Earth's populations must evolve to achieve a higher spiritual level.

According to some contactees, aliens do not make public contact with humans because Earth's karma, rooted in its main institutions, creates barriers.

Negative karma prevents aliens from contacting governments and major terrestrial institutions.

According to many historians of religion, the Space Brothers and the contactees' stories share characteristics with the Mahatmas of the Theosophical belief system.

This is true not only in terms of behavior and intentions but also in how their physical appearance is described.

The cosmology conveyed by the contactees also closely resembles that of Theosophy.

For example, the gospel of cosmic brotherhood and peace, central to the contactees' message, aligns closely with Theosophy.

Finally, the role of contactees mirrors that of Theosophical leaders, as, in the world of Theosophy, only a select minority could receive messages from the Adepts, and it was their duty to share what they had learned with others.

Moreover, Theosophical leaders were tasked with being both preachers and guardians of the Mahatmas' daily message, just as contactees are responsible for conveying the messages of the Space Brothers to humanity.

Thus, we can say that through the contactees, the traditional belief system of Theosophy was translated into a more modern language suitable for the space-age audience, which undoubtedly draws the interest of historians of religion.

Giovanni Pellegrino

My first sighting occurred when I was about ten years old. A small triangular object hovered roughly ten meters above my friend's head. It remained there for a few minutes, then slowly ascended vertically before suddenly darting away at an incredible speed. Strangely enough, this sighting was not the catalyst for my interest in ufology. From a young age, I have always been fascinated by biblical stories and their protagonists. To this day, one of my favorite films is The Ten Commandments from 1956.

I have always wondered: how could a people rebel against God? The story of Moses frequently recounts the disobedience of the Jewish people and the Egyptian Pharaoh, despite repeated divine punishments: the parting of the Red Sea, towers of fire rising into the sky, and the infamous ten plagues. How could mere humans oppose a God demonstrating such power? This was a question I pondered for years.

Over time, as I delved deeper into studying the Bible, I arrived at a conclusion: that Yahweh was not God, nor was He the only one. As the Bible itself narrates, there were other Elohim, some even more powerful than Him. So, who were these Elohim? This question was the turning point that led me to become a ufologist.

Since taking up ufology, I have focused not only on the study of sacred texts but also on abduction experiences and contactism. I have had the opportunity to interview dozens upon dozens of witnesses to such experiences, forming wonderful friendships with many of them that have lasted for years now.

In this book, we present everything related to the world of contactism and explore how it has influenced human civilization from its very beginnings. There is a strong likelihood of a significant correlation between contactism, religion, the great geniuses of our history, and the progress of civilization.

Another aspect addressed in this work is the difficulty contactees face in their daily lives. Often overlooked, even by professionals in the field, is the discomfort these individuals experience in dealing with even the simplest aspects of life. Contactees must contend with humanity's inability to comprehend what is unconventional. Ridicule, misunderstandings, and even social exclusion are part of the everyday reality for many contactees.

It is far too easy to label someone living a reality different from ours as crazy or psychotic. Thomas Edison once shared that as a child, his teacher handed him a letter to be delivered only to his mother. As she read the letter aloud, tears filled her eyes. The letter stated: "Your son is a genius. This school is not suitable for him, and the teachers are not qualified enough to educate him. Please, teach him yourself."

Years later, after his mother's death, Edison found the letter by chance and read it. The actual message was: "Your son has mental issues. Unfortunately, he can no longer attend our school. He is expelled." Edison was deeply moved and wrote in his journal: "I was a mentally ill child; my mother turned me into a genius".

Giuseppe Corcione

A BRIEF HISTORY OF CONTACTISM

Contactism is a phenomenon older than one might think, as there have always been individuals claiming to be in contact with beings not of this world. Initially, people claimed contact with angelic or spiritual religious entities. Some of these individuals created or attempted to create a religion or sect centered around the contactee, who acted as a spiritual leader. It is worth noting that many contactees of the ufological era followed a similar pattern.

The first to specifically claim contact with alien beings was Emanuel Swedenborg, a science enthusiast who, in 1744, began having visions of extraordinary beings and places on other planets, which he documented in his writings. He described the aliens as human-like, living in magnificently decorated palaces. Their external brilliance, he said, reflected their inner radiance, and their language was highly concise. Additionally, they communicated telepathically and, during the golden age, had a close bond with our ancestors, speaking to them directly.

In 1758, Swedenborg published a book recounting his travels to the planets of our solar system, stopping at Saturn, the last known planet at the time. Later, the famous Helena Blavatsky echoed similar ideas. In 1891, Thomas Blatt published a book claiming to have met an inhabitant of Mars in Kentucky, who spoke English. In 1900, Theodore Flournoy published a book detailing the claims of Héléne Smith, a medium who, while in a trance, shared information about her visit to Mars, including its alphabet and language.

In 1930, William Magoo published a book asserting he had been taken to Mars. He described the planet as similar to Earth, with cities and deserts, inhabited by beings who had radios and cars, although they were invisible. At the time, it was still unclear whether Mars was inhabited, and some scientists speculated about the possibility of life there.

In 1935, Vaillant claimed to have met aliens from Venus in a cave under Mount Shasta. He described them playing music and using a mirror-like device to show him images of life on Venus. The Venetians shared spiritual messages and predicted negative events for Earth, followed by an era of peace. Vaillant became wealthy and famous after founding an organization for his followers. This organization evolved into a religious sect, drawing millions of adherents, and Vaillant acted not only as a contactee but also as a spiritual leader, spreading the doctrine of Theosophy a precursor to the New Age movement.

Until then, contactee doctrines did not mention UFOs or flying saucers, as the era of flying saucers began only after 1947. Thus, it was not yet possible to incorporate UFOs into contactee narratives. In 1952, George Adamski initiated a series of contacts involving aliens arriving on Earth aboard flying saucers. A devoted follower of Theosophy, Adamski spoke extensively about encounters with inhabitants of other planets, as well as space and planetary travels. At the time, it was still unclear what conditions existed on Venus, Mars, or the hidden side of the Moon. Adamski supported his accounts with photographs and films that garnered public interest during that historical period. He also sold an impressive number of books, gaining fame and influence.

After Adamski, countless other contactees emerged, recounting similar stories about human-like cosmic brothers from planets within our solar system, which at the time were still thought to be potentially habitable. However, once it became evident that planets in our solar system were not habitable, contactees claimed the aliens originated beyond the solar system, beginning with Alpha Centauri. Later, when it became clear that these exoplanetary systems were also uninhabitable, contactees shifted the aliens' origins to other dimensions or parallel universes.

In the 1950s and 1960s, many contactees claimed telepathic communication with aliens, often creating organizations that attracted numerous followers and considerable notoriety. An interesting case is Billy Meyer, who claimed that by 1975, there were 17,422 contactees spread across every nation. Notably, even prominent ufologists like Timothy Good were associated with contactism. The famous Ummo case, for example, involved a form of contactism based on close encounters through postal correspondence.

In Italy, numerous contactees replicated details from American counterparts, often attempting to create ufological-religious movements by merging ufological concepts with Christian ideas and referencing the return of Jesus. Prominent figures include Eugenio Siragusa and his disciples, Giorgio Bongiovanni and Maurizio Cavallo. Bongiovanni became known as the "stigmatized contactee." Another noteworthy figure is Antonio Urzi, a follower of Bongiovanni, who described himself as "a simple instrument of Heaven in the service of Giorgio Bongiovanni and Christic truth."

The French contactee Claude Vorilhon, later known as Rael, founded a widely followed religion based on his contactee experiences. Modern contactees like these have managed to gather significant followings, often blending spirituality with ufology. Contactism also provides opportunities to sell books and attract personal recognition by creating a community of followers.

However, why do some individuals claim to be contactees without earning significant money? The answer likely lies in the prestige and power derived from convincing others of their contactee status, which can sometimes outweigh financial gain. It is important to note that many well-known ufologists have been skeptical of contactees' claims.

We conclude this overview of contactism by mentioning the notable case of Mexican contactee Carlos Diaz, who gained international attention. Diaz discovered a passageway for certain UFOs, enabling him to capture spectacular photos and videos of them. These visuals brought him popularity and lifted him out of poverty. Diaz later recounted direct interactions with aliens. While some researchers consider his photos entirely fabricated, others regard them as authentic.

With that, this brief exploration of the phenomenon of contactism comes to an end.

As everyone knows, Emanuel Swedenborg was a Swedish mystic and scientist. In the early part of his life, he became a prominent scientist and inventor, with interests spanning chemistry, anatomy, mathematics, mineralogy, and astronomy. Additionally, he was proficient in several foreign languages. At the age of 56, he entered the spiritual phase of his life, during which he experienced mystical visions of an otherworldly realm.

Swedenborg believed he was communicating with angels and spirits, including many biblical figures. From that point onward, he devoted himself to theology. The mystic revealed that these spirits guided his interpretation of the Holy Scriptures and claimed to be one of the few individuals capable of dialoguing with spirits and celestial entities from Heaven. He authored more than 50 books, most of them in Latin. Notably, only Heaven and Hell and Conversations with Angels have been translated into Italian, along with a few excerpts from other works.

Here, I would like to focus on Swedenborg's biblical, theological, and eschatological concepts. It is worth noting that his philosophy broadly aligns with a form of Christianity centered on the doctrine of correspondences between the spiritual and natural worlds. However, we will focus on three references to extraterrestrial life in Heaven and Hell, attempting to relate these reflections to certain scenarios in ufology. I want to emphasize that our discussion is in no way intended to be disrespectful or blasphemous.

Let us consider the first of the three passages, in which we allow Swedenborg to speak for himself:

"I have been told by angels that the Lord appears in heaven as the Sun... The Lord appears not in heaven but above the heavens; not overhead or at the zenith, but before the faces of angels, at a median height between the zenith and the horizon. He appears in two different ways: before the right eye as a fiery Sun similar to the Sun's fire, and before the left eye as a Moon with a brightness resembling that of the Moon on our Earth, the brightest and of a similar size. However, this Moon is surrounded by many smaller moons, all luminous and radiant. The Lord appears in these two forms because He manifests according to the reception each has of Him, that is, whether He is perceived through the goodness of love or the goodness of faith. He appears as a fiery Sun to those who perceive Him with love and as a bright, white Moon to those who perceive Him through faith."

This passage is particularly interesting from a ufological perspective. It describes the blazing Sun and, notably, the Moon surrounded by smaller moons. These images evoke similar depictions in the Old and New Testaments, interpreted by some scholars in a "clipeological" key as evidence of extraterrestrial beings visiting Earth in ancient times. According to certain authors, the spacecraft of these aliens were compared to radiant suns, meteors, luminous celestial bodies, shields, chariots, or burning beams.

Some ufologists argue that these descriptions also echo solar phenomena associated with Marian apparitions. This passage contains surprising connections to modern ufology, almost as if Swedenborg were describing glowing UFOs similar to those witnessed by countless individuals from 1947 to today. Such objects have also been sighted, albeit less frequently, in earlier historical periods, including prehistory.

However, it is important to acknowledge that this interpretation of Swedenborg's words is not the only possible one. The Swedish mystic may have been describing an otherworldly image or alluding to metaphysical concepts, using visual metaphors akin to those employed by poets and mystics referencing the supernatural something inherently ineffable in human language.

Now, let us examine two additional passages from Swedenborg, starting with paragraph 321 of Heaven and Hell, which contains the following statements:

"There are a great many inhabited earths in the universe. Only some of their inhabitants know that the Lord took on the human body on this earth, but since they worship the Divine, they are immediately accepted by the Lord."

In paragraph 417, Swedenborg writes:

"One can see how vast the Lord's heaven is from the fact that all the visible planets of our solar system are earths: these and countless other planets in the universe are all inhabited... The inhabitants of these planets, too, become spirits and angels if they live according to love and truth. There are no fewer than a million inhabited earths in the universe, each with millions of inhabitants for hundreds and hundreds of generations. However, the angels have told me that all this is nothing compared to the immensity of the Lord and His creation."

These passages seem to expand upon the verse from the Fourth Gospel: "In my Father's house, there are many mansions." Swedenborg's descriptions create a grand image of a boundless universe teeming with life, where inhabitants can ascend to the sublime divine dimension from which everything originates. These ideas bear a striking resemblance to testimonies and beliefs describing the universe as a reality filled with numerous civilizations, generally superior to humanity in ethical terms.

Swedenborg's references to life on various planets align his exobiology with the claims of contactees from the 1950s onward about inhabitants of Venus, Saturn, and other celestial bodies. While modern cosmology has largely debunked the idea that planets in our solar system host civilizations, we must not forget that some visitors, if not lying about their origins, could come from the future or parallel planetary dimensions.

In conclusion, alien civilizations might exist on planets in our solar system, albeit in parallel dimensions or within a temporal context belonging to the distant past or future.

Helen Smith claimed to have made numerous astral journeys to the planet Mars using her mediumistic abilities. In the Swiss medium's accounts, we find an interesting description of the planet Mars and its inhabitants. For the Theosophists, Mars was one of the planets where the process of reincarnation for all humanity was to continue in spiritual evolution toward perfection. Helen Smith first met Astanè on Mars, described by the Swiss woman as an illustrious man. Astanè used his magical powers to connect with the medium across space and time. Helen was particularly influenced by Theosophical concepts, which were shaped by an evolutionary logic borrowed from Darwinian theory. Infinite cycles of reincarnation, drawn from Buddhism, merged with the modern positivism of late 19th-century official science.

But how did Helen describe the planet Mars? According to the medium, it is an attractive world, more advanced than Earth, where futuristic carriages circulate without wheels or horses. Helen, in addition to describing the planet Mars in great detail, also claimed to be able to speak the Martian language. Flournoy, the psychologist from the University of Geneva, who studied the Martian language used by Helen during the mediumistic sessions, argued that this presumed Martian language was created by the medium unconsciously, resembling the early stages of languages considered from an evolutionary perspective.

However, other scholars disagreed with Flournoy. These scholars argued that a structured language like Martian with a codified script, coherent grammar, verb endings, nouns and adjectives with masculine and feminine gender, singular and plural numbers, regularly conjugated verbs, and more could not be an unconscious creation. Additionally, elements from Oriental languages, often Sanskrit, occasionally emerged in Martian, Ultramartian, and Uranian. Many scholars noted that Helen had a strong interest in languages and, unusually for a 19th-century shop assistant, took regular lessons in English and German. Other scholars who analyzed Helen's Martian language observed that it was somewhat incoherent and jumbled, which should not be too surprising given that Helen spoke Martian while in a trance.

Now we will dedicate some space to the extraterrestrial visions of the Swiss medium. How did these Martian visions come to Helen? It all began unexpectedly during a séance on October 28, 1894, when the medium met a widow who had recently lost her son. Naturally, the widow hoped the medium could provide her with some message from her son. The following month, after the usual bouts of nausea and the sensation of floating, Helen saw a star that grew until it loomed over the house where the séance was taking place. She claimed to see three planets and asked the table where she was, and the table replied, "On Mars."

The medium saw vehicles without wheels or horses gliding quickly, scattering sparks. Additionally, water fountains spouted from the rooftops of houses. Helen saw that inside a house, there was a beautiful cradle with a metallic angel with open wings instead of a curtain. It is worth noting that the Martians did not differ in appearance from Earthlings, except that they dressed in unisex clothing, with wide trousers and a tightly fitted blouse, gathered at the waist in an Oriental style.

On February 2, 1896, during a mediumistic trance, Helen spoke at length with a woman who wanted to invite her aboard a small, strange carriage, again without wheels or horses. Helen grew irritated because the woman, who initially addressed her in French, then spoke in an incomprehensible language. Helen later realized that the unknown language used by the woman was indeed Martian. Soon after, during the séance, Helen also began to speak the

Martian language. Following this, the medium began to mimic gestures of Martian courtesy broad and complex hand and finger movements accompanied by bows of various kinds. The medium then began sighing through sobs and finally fell into a deep sleep, speaking words in the Martian language.

Flournoy, who was attending the séance, gently invited her to speak French, but she, annoyed by the request, continued to speak in Martian. On September 5, 1896, Helen awoke at 3:15 a.m., troubled by an approaching storm. She sat at the foot of her bed and suddenly had a vision of a strange landscape filled with peculiar figures. She recounted being on the shore of a beautiful pink-blue Martian lake, over which stretched a yellow bridge made of transparent material resembling organ pipes. The Martian soil was peach-pink, and the women present wore flat hats similar to tableware.

On the bridge stood a dark-skinned man, Astanè, who took on the role of Helen's guide on Mars. During the séance on November 2, 1896, Helen Smith, while in a mediumistic trance, suddenly began speaking, saying she was on Mars. On the planet, she heard people speaking in Martian and understood everything they were saying. Still during this séance, Helen described the exterior of Astanè's house, including plants with leaves, soil, mountains, red walls (the typical color of Mars), and plants with purple-colored leaves. Astanè's house had windows with trumpet-shaped frames in dark red, turquoise curtains, and an unusual yellow roof.

Astanè stepped forward, appearing as a yellow-skinned man dressed entirely in white. The houses around him were painted in contrasting colors, with bright blue curtains. During the same séance, Helen described another Martian scene: a green lake with gray-colored shores. Tall yellow spires with edges and peaks decorated with pink and blue spheres rose high. The surrounding hills were pink, while the vegetation, resembling Earth's, was predominantly green. The buildings had red edges and pinnacles, while the window curtains were turquoise. Yellow spires adorned the rooftops, along with beautiful red crenellations.

In this setting, Martians wearing wide white hats and red or dark clothing wandered about. Helen's guide, Astanè, was often accompanied by a bothersome and mischievous creature that frightened Helen. The medium also described seeing hideous aquatic creatures resembling enormous snails, which Astanè caught with iron fishing rods. During the séance on November 28, 1897, the usual red halo that preceded Martian visions appeared. On that occasion, Helen saw a street on Mars illuminated by lamps mounted on buildings. Inside one house, she saw a large, beautiful, brightly lit square hall adorned with lovely plants.

In the hall, many aliens dressed in Martian fashion wandered about: beautiful girls with long braids falling down their backs, adorned with pink butterflies on their heads. The Martians were preparing to eat, and Helen noted that the plates on the table were square and the goblets resembled teacups. A waiter brought to the table, on a large tray, a cooked animal resembling a cat. The vision of the Martian meal abruptly ended, but Helen managed to see Astanè hosting the gathering, carving the roast for his guests.

How can we interpret Helen Smith's astral journeys to Mars in light of Theosophy and the social atmosphere of late 19th-century Geneva? Theosophy held that the path to spiritual perfection continued on other planets in the solar system, according to a pseudo-Darwinian logic. Helen Smith was notably interested in Theosophy.

What about the Martian language Helen used in some of her mediumistic séances? Flournoy rightly pointed out that Helen's Martian was a genuine language, composed of clearly articulated sounds, well-defined words, and stable, consistent meanings, similar to terrestrial languages. Flournoy also noted that, at times, in Helen's Martian, the same letter represented multiple sounds or that different letters corresponded to the same sound something that also occurs in languages like English.

Finally, the Geneva psychologist observed that the intonation with which the medium pronounced words in Martian differed from European languages. Flournoy described it as a high tone, similar to Chinese, reflecting the tonal nature common to many Eastern languages, where high and low tones alternate to create meaning a concept unfamiliar to European languages, which rely on sounds rather than intonation.

In conclusion, we note that Helen's Martian language also possessed a meaningful grammar.

THE ASTRAL TRAVELS TO ULTRA-MARS AND URANUS BY HELEN SMITH

Helen did not limit herself to astral journeys only to Mars but claimed to have visited other planets in our solar system, namely Ultra-Mars and Uranus. Therefore, there was not only a Martian cycle but also an Ultra-Martian and Uranian cycle. The Ultra-Martian cycle began sporadically in the autumn of 1898 and can be said to have merged with the tail end of the Martian cycle, of which it was a natural continuation.

However, the full unfolding of Ultra-Mars and its language occurred in 1900, just before Smith, deeply offended by the publication of Flournoy's book From India to the Planet Mars, publicly repudiated Flournoy, whom she had previously idealized and loved as a surrogate father. Helen repudiated Flournoy because, after reading his book, she realized that the Geneva psychologist had considered her a clinical case to study. As a result, while Flournoy can still provide much information about Helen's travels to Ultra-Mars and even Uranus, he can say nothing about her lunar journeys, as she no longer trusted him and had severed their relationship.

During the Martian cycle, a new guide suddenly appeared named Raniè, who announced the medium's transfer to another planet. On October 22, 1898, Helen woke up around 6 a.m. and began sewing. The light suddenly dimmed, and total darkness fell. While an invisible arm grasped her waist, a pink light appeared. This light was usually the prelude to Martian visions, so Helen immediately grabbed pen and paper.

Next to her appeared an individual with a Martian appearance and attire. This figure was Raniè, who moments earlier, while still invisible, had encircled her waist. At that moment, the alien pointed to a panel that was not entirely clear and visible. The man spoke phrases in a language she did not immediately understand. However, Helen faithfully transcribed the words she heard. This was the announcement of her arrival on Ultra-Mars.

At that moment, Helen saw a patch of land populated by numerous aliens of very short stature, about 80 cm tall.

These aliens had black fingernails and very large feet, and the Ultra-Martians wore shoes. Helen saw no vegetation, at least not in the limited space she could observe. Instead of houses, the medium saw strange, low, long huts without doors or windows. These Ultra-Martian huts featured a small covered gallery that served as an entrance. Their roofs were flat, with chimneys and vents on top. The ground was barren and almost black, with no roads or sidewalks. In short, everything Helen observed seemed crude and primitive.

The Ultra-Martians were bare-chested, with exposed arms, and wore a sort of narrow skirt cinched at the waist, held up by unusual suspenders. These beings had tiny, completely shaved heads, short necks, microscopic eyes, very wide mouths, and strangely shaped noses. The Ultra-Martians spoke to each other in a mysterious language, with heads twice as wide as the height of their bodies. Shortly after, the vision disappeared, and Helen felt her right hand controlled by an external force, pushing her to draw strange, unfamiliar characters.

But what were the characteristics of Ultra-Mars? This new planet was a strange world inhabited by coarse, almost animal-like creatures dwarves with heads twice the width of their bodies. In short, Ultra-Mars was a planet lagging on the evolutionary scale. As a result, Ultra-Mars and its language reflected this fact. Unlike Mars, Ultra-Mars bore no resemblance to Earth, and its language consisted only of words ending in consonants.

One day, while Helen was taking a day off, another vision occurred, undoubtedly significant. Suddenly, rosy rays filled her home, gradually darkening in color. The medium once again saw a desolate natural environment and primitive-looking aliens. Two of these aliens were engaged in an intense conversation. While listening to this conversation, Helen found herself inside a neglected, rough house with a strange suspended shelf that reached up to the ceiling, resembling a bed. Confirming this idea, an inhabitant of Ultra-Mars lay down to rest on it.

However, Helen's vision did not end there, as she noticed a crude relief on a nearby wall made of dried mud, depicting an ugly and threatening face. This was a deity of the planet Ultra-Mars, which Helen drew. This deity closely resembled the threatening faces of Inca and Aztec idols. In a mediumistic session a few days later, the medium drew what she saw: Ultra-Martian insects. These insects were so numerous that they seemed like a genuine invasion.

Helen had another vision in broad daylight while at work. During this vision, she saw letters of the Ultra-Martian alphabet but could not write down any words that appeared. However, the following evening, she suddenly heard a phrase spoken in the Ultra-Martian language.

On May 27, 1900, during a mediumistic session at home, Helen, in a trance, traveled to another planet and saw Martian graphic symbols in the form of sudden flashes. She fell into a deeper trance and wrote Ultra-Martian hieroglyphs, which she later translated into Martian words. Not long after, on June 17, 1900, the medium, in a trance, traveled to another planet, Uranus. Upon reaching Uranus, she described in a semi-dream state what she saw: three suns, one behind the other, stunning to behold, which filled her with ecstasy and wonder.

The houses on Uranus were truly unique, resembling long chimneys connected by small bridges that rose on one side and descended on the other. The Uranian aliens Helen saw were exclusively male, nearly bald, and short in stature, with unusually short fingers. Their clothing was also peculiar: tight-fitting sleeves and a wide bodice that fell straight to the knees.

Helen described Ultra-Martian as the language of a primitive population that had not yet developed a proper alphabet. Like early Earth civilizations, the Ultra-Martians wrote their language using ideograms. However, the Geneva medium believed that the Ultra-Martians had achieved a certain level of cultural evolution, as their ideograms were no longer purely pictographic but had acquired symbolic refinement, similar to the development of Egyptian writing.

According to Helen, the Ultra-Martian language consisted of about 100 words. Like Martian, it had a high-pitched intonation, distinct from European languages. Flournoy described Ultra-Martian as a somber language. Some authors noted poetic elements in Ultra-Martian, as seen in Martian. Helen also translated Ultra-Martian into Martian.

Skeptical authors believe that Helen's creation of Martian, Ultra-Martian, and Uranian languages originated from autosuggestion. They argue that these languages were consciously fabricated, drawing from French and other ancient and modern languages Helen knew. Conversely, proponents of Helen's paranormal abilities emphasize that creating languages like Martian, Ultra-Martian, and Uranian from scratch was no easy task. Finally, they note that while these alien languages were not always consistent or entirely authentic, no language on Earth is perfect.

In the past twenty years, the New Age movement has significantly increased its number of adherents, causing considerable concern within the Catholic Church. From the perspective of the historian of religions, New Age is a Gnostic and neopagan movement, while from a sociological standpoint, it can be described as a network of people who share the same beliefs and worldview. Since belief in aliens is a fundamental aspect of New Age doctrines, it is fair to say that the overwhelming success of New Age is one of the sociological causes of the interest in UFOs observable in the modern world. With this in mind, we will attempt to describe the fundamental elements of New Age ufology.

In the New Age phenomenon, over the past thirty years, the conception of UFOs has changed significantly, shifting from a material understanding to an idea of UFOs emphasizing the spiritual aspects inherent in ufological phenomenology. Many members of the New Age claim to have had contact with aliens without any physical encounters with them. Aquarians assert that it is possible to travel among the stars and meet aliens through "thoughts," "emotions," and, most importantly, by using astral travel.

In Aquarian circles, there is a strong emphasis on investigating the "soft" aspects of the UFO phenomenon. This investigation is said to occur on a non-physical level, using not the five senses but the astral body. In summary, New Age affirms that it is possible to meet aliens and study UFOs by moving into the astral dimension. In this dimension, one could encounter various entities, including extraterrestrials.

Consequently, for Aquarians, it is unnecessary to physically meet aliens or enter UFOs to travel through space; the ability to perform astral travel suffices. Moreover, according to New Age, it is possible to visit the planets where aliens come from by moving into the astral dimension. Some New Age writers claim to have received important information about the culture, religion, and social structures on various planets inhabited by extraterrestrial civilizations.

However, beyond astral travel, there is, according to New Age, another way to contact aliens, known as channeling, which is essentially a modern form of spiritualism in which mediums not only encounter spirits but also fairies, gnomes, angels, and extraterrestrials. Many Aquarians use channeling to contact aliens, and numerous books have been written by New Age adherents who feel obliged to share the messages they have received from aliens.

It is worth noting that the idea that mediums can contact extraterrestrials is not new, contrary to what many New Age writers claim. In fact, as early as the 19th century, the idea was widespread that mediums could be possessed by extraterrestrial spirits and, consequently, could receive information about aliens. For example, a 19th-century medium, Helene Smith, claimed to have been in contact with Martians and wrote several books she called the "Martian cycle." According to the medium, the unknown language in which these books were written was the language spoken on Mars.

But what is the essence of the messages that Aquarians claim to receive from aliens through channeling? Generally, the content of these messages is similar to what was conveyed by the contactees of the 1950s. In that era, some contactees placed particular emphasis on religious messages. In most cases, the content of these messages is repetitive, banal, and lacking in internal coherence. Nevertheless, despite the limitations of the messages received through channeling, they often allow recipients to gain a degree of popularity and even to write books that achieve considerable success.

We do not wish to delve into overly complex sociological considerations to explain this fact, which would not surprise a sociologist. However, we want to highlight that the success of a theory, a book, or a new prophet often does not depend on the internal coherence of its messages but on a sociological variable called "social desirability." Simply put, there are ideas, beliefs, interpretations of facts, and ideals that are favored by public opinion. Sometimes, this happens independently of the presence or absence of objective reasons to justify such attitudes. These ideal attitudes and beliefs have high social desirability and, for this reason, succeed even when they occasionally support nonsensical or contradictory ideas.

Returning to channeling, we must note that it allows for an "inflation of relations" with the dimension of the "Supra" (religious historians consider the Supra to include all beings deemed superior to humans). For New Age ufology, aliens are also considered "Cosmic Masters" and, as such, spiritually superior to humans, thus belonging to the dimension of the Supra. We believe that channeling has caused an "inflation of relations with the Supra" because today, a significant number of people claim to have relations with superior beings, including aliens, through channeling.

Some even claim to have received missions from these superior beings to help humanity. According to New Age ufology, aliens also entrust important missions to many New Age adherents, who then become "new prophets of the aliens." We wish to conclude the discussion of New Age ufology by summarizing the main ideas of Brad Steiger, its most prominent figure. Steiger claims that aliens are helping humans adapt to the needs of the New Age, or the Age of Aquarius. To this end, Steiger explains in various books that extraterrestrials are reincarnating on Earth to live among humans. According to him, the most prominent figures in the New Age are aliens who have agreed to reincarnate on Earth, even though they lack a clear memory of their extraterrestrial origins.

However, Steiger asserts that these aliens can become aware of their extraterrestrial origins through hypnotic regression or meditation. These aliens, who have agreed to reincarnate on Earth, allegedly have important missions to accomplish on our planet. Various proponents of New Age ufology have adopted and expanded Steiger's theories. One of the most significant innovations is that aliens not only reincarnate on Earth but also enter the bodies of adult humans, taking control of their minds. Prominent New Age figures even claim to have undergone a sudden personality change because aliens have taken possession of their minds.

Research conducted by various historians of religions has shown that, in both Europe and the United States, a considerable number of New Age adherents believe they are of alien origin or are possessed by aliens. As we can see from what we have described, belief in aliens is of paramount importance in the New Age.

CONSIDERATIONS ON THE UMMO AFFAIR

Ummo is a hypothetical exoplanet from which the "Ummites" civilization is said to originate. Some representatives of the highest organization of Ummo are believed to have contacted Earthlings through a long series of letters and typewritten documents. These letters and documents were allegedly sent by mail to individuals interested in the UFO phenomenon. The Ummo case gained some popularity in Spain and France during the 1960s and 1970s. The authors of these letters presented themselves as members of an extraterrestrial civilization from Ummo, who had come to Earth to conduct scientific research. Most scholars consider the Ummo affair to lack credibility.

In 1993, José Luis Peña, an engineer and psychology scholar, claimed to be the author of all the "Ummite" letters. However, many ufologists consider it unlikely that a single person could have organized and managed such a complex hoax over several decades. In 1966 and 1967, there was a first wave of letters sent primarily, but not exclusively, to Fernando Sesma Manzano, a Spanish civil servant. In subsequent years, the number of letters sent decreased, while the number of recipients increased, until the second half of the 1980s, when there was a second wave of letters with different content, less technical and more philosophical. The first letters were received in January 1966.

According to historian Mike Dash, the Ummo affair began on February 6, 1966, in Madrid, the day when engineer Peña claimed to have witnessed a UFO in Aluche. According to the witness, it was a large circular object with three legs and a curious symbol on the underside three vertical lines joined by a horizontal line. This was the same symbol the Ummites used to stamp their letters. Peña's account caused a certain stir, but it was only the beginning.

Shortly afterward, in Madrid, the author of a book on UFOs received many photographs in an anonymous envelope depicting a UFO similar to the one described by Peña, including the same symbol. According to Dash's reconstruction, a few weeks after the Aluche sighting, Fernando Sesma Manzano received several typewritten letters claiming to be from an extraterrestrial race originating from the planet Ummo. Within the year, various individuals, particularly in Madrid, received about 150 Ummite documents, totaling approximately 1,000 pages. Each page of the documents bore the same symbol depicting three vertical lines joined by a horizontal one.

Subsequently, many others received Ummite letters, including French scientist Jean-Pierre Petit, who claimed to have used Ummite material in his research. The Ummo affair gained further momentum from the sighting of a UFO with the Ummo symbol in 1967 in Spain, at San Jose de Valderas. The witnesses to this sighting were traced and interviewed by Peña. However, it must be noted that few ufologists outside Spain took the Ummo affair seriously, as there were suspicions about the authenticity of the photos. Moreover, although the content of the letters was much more complex and detailed than the communications of most contactees, there was nothing definitively alien about them. Some researchers concluded that the Ummo affair was merely a hoax.

The hoax hypothesis gained particular traction in 1993, when Peña confessed to being the author of the letters, though his confession did not convince all scholars. In June 2002, a French scientist, writing under the pseudonym Jean Pollion, published a book analyzing the Ummite language, concluding that it was different from all other known languages. The true identity of the author behind the pseudonym Jean Pollion remains unknown.

It must be noted that, following the Ummite claims, small groups of Ummite adherents were also formed. One scholar even compiled a dictionary of the Ummo language. Regarding the content of the Ummite letters, two of them recount the arrival of the Ummites on Earth, which allegedly took place on March 28, 1950. A small group of extraterrestrial scientists is said to have landed to study our planet and culture. The Earth was reportedly discovered by the Ummites after intercepting a telegraph message sent in February 1934 by a Norwegian navigator off the coast of Newfoundland.

Other letters describe the living conditions on the planet Ummo, with numerous illustrations. These describe daily life, work, family, entertainment, art, education, and sexuality. Other Ummite letters discuss their history, the systems of government that have existed on Ummo, and the current political system. The Ummites describe their current political system as "socialist." Another part of the letters deals with philosophy, metaphysics, and religion. In many letters, the concept of God is discussed. Furthermore, those who have studied the Ummite letters have highlighted that their concept of God has similarities with the Christian one.

Many other letters contain detailed scientific topics, including the theory of the unified field and subjects in astrophysics, cosmology, biology, and evolution. In their messages, the Ummites claim to come from the planet Ummo, located about 14 light-years from Earth and orbiting the star Umma, identified with the red dwarf Wolff 424 in the Virgo constellation. The term the Ummites use to refer to themselves in their language is Seminii. In their letters, the Ummites provide many details about their language, civilization, customs, and traditions, using many words in the Ummite language. Additionally, they provide precise explanations of the meanings of these words and their possible phonetic transcription into Spanish.

One significant issue regarding the Ummo affair is the identity of the author of the Ummite letters. Three main hypotheses have been proposed: José Luis Peña, intelligence agencies, or the Ummites. Skeptics argue that typewritten letters sent by mail cannot be considered evidence of the existence of extraterrestrials. Skeptical scholars believe the letters to be more or less elaborate forgeries and suggest that Peña, alone or with an accomplice, authored the first letters. Subsequently, other individuals supposedly based their letters on these originals as a model to create a myth. Other scholars, including Spanish ufologist Manuel Carballal, have hypothesized the involvement of intelligence agencies such as the CIA or the Spanish secret service in the Ummo affair.

For other authors who support the extraterrestrial hypothesis, the letters were written by the Ummites. Authors like Spanish ufologist Antonio Ribera argue that the UFO with the Ummo symbol sighted in Spain at San Jose de Valderas and landed in the nearby town of Santa Monica presents too many favorable elements to be dismissed as a simple hoax. These favorable elements include the witnesses, the photos, and the discovery of a particular plastic material at the landing site. According to other authors, one element supporting the extraterrestrial hypothesis is the scientific information contained in the letters, which allegedly surpasses terrestrial knowledge. Among the proponents of the extraterrestrial hypothesis, we should mention Jean-Pierre Petit.

We conclude this article by noting that, from a scientific perspective, the most controversial statement in the Ummite letters concerns the distance of the Wolff 424 star around which the planet Ummo is said to orbit. One of the first letters reports a distance of 3.68 light-years, consistent with measurements made in 1938 but not with the more accurate ones conducted in 1952, which determined the distance to be 14.3 light-years. After the error was pointed out, the Ummites clarified in a subsequent letter that the difference between these two values was due to fluctuations in the structure of space-time.

In summary, the Ummo case represents an intriguing example of the UFO phenomenon, addressing complex themes such as belief in contact with extraterrestrial civilizations and the sociological and religious implications of such experiences. Despite the debate over the veracity of the letters and the identity of their authors, the fascination exerted by Ummo and the Ummite civilization continues to captivate scholars and UFO enthusiasts, leaving open questions about humanity's place in the universe and the possibility of life beyond our planet.

THE CONTACTEES FROM THE PERSPECTIVE OF THE HISTORY OF RELIGIONS AND THE SOCIOLOGY OF RELIGION

In the following pages, we will focus on ufological religions, namely, those religions born from the messages received by contactees individuals who claim to have met aliens and received from them the mission of communicating truths of fundamental importance to humanity. Essentially, we will discuss contactees using the frameworks of the history of religions and the sociology of religion.

To begin, it is essential to note that modern accounts of encounters between humans and non-human entities from other worlds belong to an ancient tradition rooted in the depths of time. A particularly striking observation is the similarity between the stories told by contactees and the doctrines of theosophy since the space brothers share the same characteristics as the cosmic masters within the theosophical system. Moreover, theosophy asserted that the planets of our solar system were inhabited and that humans reincarnated on these planets to complete their spiritual evolutionary journey.

It is also worth mentioning that it is not difficult to categorize contactees within well-defined sociological and historical religious typologies. They share much in common with other types of prophets, and the structure of their belief systems closely resembles those found in many conventional religions. In fact, contactees can be considered the prophets of the space age, akin to the prophets of the Judeo-Christian tradition, and can be understood within the broader context of a Weberian "prophetic pattern."

In this regard, Max Weber distinguishes between two types of prophets: emissary prophets and exemplary prophets. Contactees fit the emissary type, as this kind of prophet believes they have received an important message that must be communicated to humanity. Additionally, contactees can be placed into other religious models. For example, many claims and beliefs of contactees resemble shamanism. Shamans journey to the spirit world, where they gain powers and knowledge to bring back and use to benefit humans. Similarly, many contactees travel through space to distant worlds, witness various wonders, and return to Earth wiser, intending to assist humanity.

Furthermore, contactees share many characteristics with spiritist mediums; indeed, some use channeling, a modern form of spiritism. Channeling holds significant importance in the history of new religions, not just ufological ones, as it allows for continuous revelation and establishes a unique relationship with the supernatural realm. Returning to contactees, most demonstrate a profound interest in magic and esotericism subjects studied within the history of religions and the sociology of religion.

Notably, before becoming contactees, some individuals experienced paranormal phenomena, enabling them to have visions of various entities. In some cases, phenomena like poltergeist activity (unexplained noises, lights, or the movement of objects and furniture) occur in the homes of contactees, sometimes only after the person becomes a contactee. In other instances, the contactee reports having always had a special relationship with the paranormal.

From what has been stated so far, it is evident that there is a mysterious link between paranormal and mediumistic abilities and the potential to become a contactee. Another common characteristic of many contactees is the belief that they are predestined individuals, chosen by aliens from birth to fulfill a specific mission. Naturally, considering oneself an elect has significant implications for the personality of contactees.

A psychological trait often observed among contactees is their conviction that their mission is hindered by the ignorance and malevolence of others, or even by conspiracies, which aim to prevent them from sharing the will of extraterrestrials with humanity. It should be noted that the figure of the persecuted prophet opposed by wicked and impious people frequently appears in the history of many religions. For example, in Judaism, many prophets were persecuted for persistently proclaiming God's word in a hostile environment.

Another characteristic common to nearly all contactees is their uncritical acceptance of the messages they receive from aliens. Consequently, contactees often fail to recognize the contradictions within the messages they are entrusted with. A recurring theme in the contactee universe is the strong tendency toward religious syncretism, as their ufological religions often integrate elements from various religious traditions. Many ufological cults blend Christian elements with aspects of neopaganism, Eastern religions, or Gnostic principles. In other words, the cosmic religions preached by contactees have two fundamental traits: first, they are presented as the completion and perfection of past religions, which are deemed no longer suitable for contemporary humans.

Second, these religions attempt to merge magical, scientific, esoteric, and religious elements, striving to reconcile even the irreconcilable. Such ideas strongly resemble those of the New Age. Notably, many contactees belong to the Aquarian movement, which views ufological religions based on channeling favorably. Another central aspect of contactees' religious vision and messages is their apocalyptic themes, asserting that Earth is in danger of destruction from natural catastrophes or nuclear conflicts caused by human malevolence. Such catastrophic events can be prevented through the intervention of extraterrestrials, who are perceived as cosmic saviors.

As a result, many ufological religions feature soteriological themes. These apocalyptic and soteriological themes are often coupled with messianic ideas, centered on the belief in an imminent public manifestation of aliens on Earth, who are seen as true cosmic messiahs. Contactees claim that this imminent alien manifestation must be prepared by the efforts of an enlightened minority their followers.

Another idea common among nearly all contactees is the necessity of abolishing nations to achieve a global government uniting all the peoples of Earth. After describing the characteristics of contactees, we will now examine the main traits found in the beliefs and behavior of their followers. Without a doubt, the most intriguing psychological trait of contactees' followers is their strong psychological dependence on the contactee.

This dependence stems both from the charisma typically associated with nearly all prophets, including contactees, and from the particular personality structure often observed in these followers. Another psychological characteristic of contactees' followers is their belief in being elect individuals, distinct from most humans. This perceived uniqueness is essentially rooted in the belief that they have been chosen by the prophet of a higher reality to carry out a specific mission, such as preparing for the arrival of aliens on Earth. Many followers of contactees are also notable for their zeal in proselytizing and missionary fervor. Furthermore, followers of contactees are often individuals disillusioned by previous religious experiences.

It is quite common for those unable to find answers to profound metaphysical questions to turn to so-called new religions, abandoning traditional major religions. This observation helps explain the proliferation of new religious movements in Western society, including ufological religions. It is important to note that the spread of new religious movements is a primary subject of study within the history of religions and the sociology of religion. These disciplines, therefore, cannot ignore the phenomenon of contactees. It must be emphasized that contactees are genuine modern prophets.

Ufologists, in turn, offer differing opinions on the credibility of the messages conveyed by contactees. Regarding the reliability of these new prophets, it is worth mentioning Jacques Vallée's "burnt-out lightbulbs" metaphor. The

Franco-American ufologist compares contactees to low-voltage lightbulbs, imagining the UFO phenomenon (the electrical current) manifesting in them with a traumatic high voltage. It becomes evident that most lightbulbs (contactees) will fail under such high voltage.

Contactees unable to withstand the trauma induced by the ufological phenomenon exhibit erratic, irrational, and contradictory behavior, making systematic studies of them futile. Conversely, contactees who can endure the high tension from their encounter with the ufological phenomenon are worthy of ufologists' attention. In conclusion, as long as contactees demonstrate a sufficiently critical attitude, scientific exploration of their messages can be considered valuable.

The most pressing issue, however, is understanding the forces and entities behind the contactee phenomenon, as this could provide deeper insight into the broader ufological phenomena.

DIFFERENCE BETWEEN A CONTACTEE AND A CONTACTED

Eugenio Siragusa was one of the most renowned Italian contactees. His activity began in the 1960s and lasted until his passing in 2006. Founder of the Cosmic Brotherhood Study Center, lecturer, and author, Siragusa left a significant legacy in the field of Italian ufology. His name is still remembered among enthusiasts of ufology and spirituality, not only in Italy but also internationally. On April 30, 1962, Siragusa was walking on Mount Manfrè (on the southern slope of Mount Etna in Sicily) when he suddenly noticed a strange glow in the sky. From this glow, a disc-shaped flying object appeared and landed nearby. Siragusa was immediately enveloped by an intense light and a profound feeling of bliss. From the disc-shaped object emerged two luminous figures, tall, human-like in appearance, and resembling the angels described in the Bible. These beings radiated an aura of love and wisdom, communicated telepathically, and identified themselves as belonging to the "Cosmic Brotherhood."

The message conveyed to Siragusa primarily focused on the destructive path humanity had taken, particularly concerning the use of nuclear weapons. The beings claimed that more evolved extraterrestrial civilizations wished to help humans avoid self-destruction and advance spiritually. This encounter led Siragusa to dedicate his life to spreading the messages he received over the years during many other encounters with extraterrestrials: messages of peace, universal love, and planetary protection.

Elizabeth Klarer was a South African contactee from the 1950s. Klarer claimed to have had an encounter with an extraterrestrial named Akon, who took her aboard his spaceship and showed her his planet a highly advanced world without wars or diseases and with profound scientific and spiritual knowledge. This alien world was called Meton, a planet orbiting in the Alpha Centauri star system. Klarer was one of the first women to recount having a sexual relationship with extraterrestrials, claiming she bore a child with Akon a son who was then raised on Meton to avoid the dangers of Earth.

Maurizio Cavallo is generally considered a contactee. His direct experiences with extraterrestrials began in the 1980s. These beings, from a planet called Clarion, were reportedly physically similar to humans but more spiritually and technologically advanced. Cavallo began his work as a communicator, writing books, participating in conferences, and sharing the messages he received from the "Space Brothers," along with numerous photographs of these beings to support the authenticity of his experiences. This activity aligns him more closely with the profile of a contactee, as he disseminates broader messages and has effectively created a small community of believers in his experiences and extraterrestrial messages.

The stories of Siragusa, Klarer, and Cavallo, summarized here, highlight the subtle difference between a contactee and a contacted individual. Essentially, all contactees are contacted individuals, but not all contacted individuals become contactees. In some cases, "contacted" can be synonymous with "contactee," referring to someone who has had contact with extraterrestrial entities. However, the term "contacted" more generally describes someone who has experienced such contact without necessarily taking on an active or mediating role. Unlike contacted individuals, who simply share their experiences without further implications, contactees tend to have a more active role: writing books, organizing conferences, forming communities, founding religious movements, or even creating new religions. A prime example is Rael (Claude Vorilhon), founder of the Raelian Movement, who in 1973 claimed to have met Yahweh, the leader of the Elohim.

In essence, contactees reach a much broader audience. Typically, a contactee views their activity as a genuine mission, dedicating their entire life to spreading messages of love, fraternity, and raising awareness about the alien phenomenon, respect for nature and the planet, peace among nations, and the irresponsible use of nuclear weapons. Regardless of the veracity of their experiences, there is no doubt about the significance of the messages they spread for humanity. Adopting the advice of aliens, or alleged aliens, would undoubtedly benefit all of humanity. Certainly, there would no longer be wars, hunger, social divisions, discrimination, violence of any kind, material attachments, and much more. If we followed the recommendations of many contactees, we would undoubtedly be better than we are today, and perhaps even ready for a massive contact event with star civilizations.

Personally, I believe that too little importance is given to the role contactees have played and continue to play in our society, as well as to their messages. Too often, the mistake is made of considering them all charlatans and painting them with the same brush. Of course, caution is needed to avoid fraudsters (who exist in all sectors), but we must also pay closer attention to those who genuinely experience such phenomena. This appeal is not only to the scientific community but also, regrettably, to many ufologists who underestimate these experiences. The role of ufologists is first and foremost to discern whether a contactee's experience is genuine, gather as much information as possible, and bring it to the attention of both the public and the scientific community.

If other forms of life exist in the universe, if these are vastly superior to us in technological and spiritual terms, and if they are in contact with some humans, then who better than contactees can help us learn more about stellar civilizations?

I deeply believe in the mission of contactees and the pivotal role they have played throughout human history. Indeed, I view contactees as central figures in humanity's story, stretching back to the dawn of time. As we will see later, in the past, the contactee was known by other names: prophet, priest, shaman, guru, genius. This does not mean believing everyone or everything certain individuals claim, nor does it mean glorifying or idolizing such individuals to the point of fanaticism, whether religious or otherwise.

Anyone preaching violence, hatred, or inequality should be considered an enemy of humanity. Always remember, no God or highly advanced extraterrestrial civilization will ever ask you to harm others in the name of a greater good. God does not kill; God gives life. God does not punish; God forgives.

THE PROGRESS OF HUMAN CIVILIZATION

History teaches us that through the discoveries and insights of brilliant individuals, humanity has made significant strides in all fields: science, mathematics, astronomy, biology, medicine, philosophy, and technology. Today, we can travel to the Moon and send probes across the universe, all thanks to the brilliant minds of the past who have gradually contributed to the progress of our civilization. But what does this have to do with contactees? Is it possible that the great minds of human history were in contact with entities not of this world, perhaps without even realizing it? Could it be that behind the major discoveries of our history lies the hand of extraterrestrials? The wealth of information received from contactees urges us not to underestimate these possibilities. One way in which aliens might assist humanity could be by suggesting ideas through dreams or visions.

Have you ever faced a challenging situation, with a seemingly unsolvable problem, and then, out of nowhere, a flash of insight comes to mind? A thought, an image, or a voice whispering the solution to you a so-called stroke of genius? This could be evidence of a connection between the physical and etheric worlds. Aliens, therefore, might use this connection to help humanity with occasional suggestions across various epochs, aiming to help us progress and evolve as a species.

I fully understand that this may sound like science fiction. However, quantum physics, with the phenomenon of entanglement, has demonstrated that information can travel instantaneously across the universe. Entanglement is a phenomenon where two particles, such as photons or electrons, remain connected even when separated by light-years, with changes in one instantaneously affecting the other. Could we hypothesize that a highly advanced civilization uses entanglement, or something similar, to remain connected and communicate with humans? It is certainly a fascinating hypothesis, though it remains speculative for now. Unfortunately, many questions remain unanswered, but this does not stop us from asking them. While the questions may seem absurd, when the answers come, they may be even more astonishing.

Starting with the Sumerians, who invented writing, the wheel, and the plow, here is a list of key inventions and discoveries that have been pivotal in humanity's journey toward understanding the world and the universe and improving living conditions. This list, though not exhaustive, includes some of the most important discoveries and inventions across various fields:

- Egyptians: With their use of papyrus, they facilitated the spread of knowledge.

- Babylonians: The Code of Hammurabi, the first written laws guaranteeing justice and rights.

- Euclid: Elements (Euclidean Geometry), the most influential work in the history of mathematics.

- Archimedes: One of history's greatest scientists, contributing to physics, engineering, and geometry. His war machines, shrouded in mystery, were said to have repelled Roman ships.

- Arabic Numbers, Decimal System, and Algebra (Al-Khwarizmi): Revolutionized mathematics and commerce.

- Compass (Chinese): Enhanced maritime navigation.

- Printing Press (Johannes Gutenberg): Enabled mass production of books and a more effective dissemination of knowledge.

- Heliocentric Theory (Nicolaus Copernicus): Revolutionized the understanding of the universe.

- Galileo Galilei: Laid the foundations of modern science.

And many more: Isaac Newton (Laws of Motion and Gravity), James Clerk Maxwell (Electromagnetism), Albert Einstein (Theory of Relativity), James Watson and Francis Crick (Structure of DNA), Robert Kahn and Vinton Cerf (Internet), genetic sequencing technology, nuclear energy, and artificial intelligence.

The Sumerians are considered the first human civilization. Their religion was polytheistic, meaning they believed in multiple deities they called the Anunnaki ("those who came down from the heavens to Earth"). According to Sumerian tablets, the Anunnaki were technologically advanced extraterrestrial beings who came from the planet Nibiru. Once on Earth, these beings supposedly modified the DNA of a terrestrial primate through genetic engineering, giving rise to human civilization with the creation of Adamu (the biblical Adam). Millennia later, Sumerian myths inspired the stories of the Old Testament, particularly Genesis.

So, is this merely a myth, or is there a truth being hidden? Was the first human civilization advanced thanks to the intervention of extraterrestrials described as deities? Why do all the great civilizations of the past recount the arrival of beings from the stars who bestowed knowledge upon humankind? Why do ancient texts from all cultures worldwide speak of godlike figures resembling humans in every way except for their immense knowledge? Anunnaki, Elohim, Theoi, Deva, Asura, Atlanteans, Neteru, and many others were they all highly evolved beings possessing technology millennia ahead of ours, yet more similar to us than we might imagine?

These beings aged, fell ill, and died (though they lived much longer than us, appearing almost immortal). They ate, slept, needed transportation (celestial chariots), quarreled, waged wars with highly advanced weapons (far more powerful than today's nuclear arms), fell in love, and felt emotions just like humans. Essentially, they shared with us strengths and weaknesses, virtues and flaws, certainties and fears. Those who would become the deities of various religions, passed down to the present day, were likely extraterrestrial beings who, in some way, contributed to the progress of human civilization through priests, shamans, prophets, philosophers, and scientists.

As previously mentioned, all myths from all cultures have strong similarities, and from these, all the world's religions were born. It's no coincidence that priests, oracles, and prophets wielded great influence over people, even affecting decisions made by leaders such as pharaohs, kings, and emperors. This power, which has persisted through millennia, continues to this day. Even though the Church has lost much of its past power, it still holds significant influence over the masses. The Vatican is considered one of the most powerful states in the world. Billions of believers across the globe, of all religions, demonstrate how that contact thousands of years ago still impacts humanity for better or worse.

Let's focus for a moment on the great minds of history the so-called geniuses, individuals with superior intellect who brought groundbreaking innovations to every field, even altering the course of history. The term genius literally means "one who communicates with divinity." In ancient times, a genius was considered a messenger of divine will; in some cultures, they were even thought to be deities themselves. Leonardo da Vinci is regarded as the greatest genius of all time, and what if he had been in contact with some higher entity without even realizing it?

LEONARDO DA VINCI

Leonardo da Vinci, born in Florence in 1452, lived during the peak of the Renaissance a period of great intellectual awakening, aimed at restoring humanism through art and intellect, marked by significant artistic and scientific achievements. Leonardo excelled in diverse fields: painting, sculpture, optics, geometry, mechanics, anatomy, geology, and much more. In 2011, the Discovery space shuttle docked with the International Space Station to deliver the last in a series of humanoid robots: Robonaut 2, a true marvel of robotic engineering. Not everyone knows that NASA engineers drew inspiration from Leonardo's illustrations for these robots. About 500 years ago, this universal genius was working on three-dimensional models that could essentially create a virtual human. But there's more: Leonardo also designed flying machines like airplanes and helicopters, as well as war machines like tanks devices that would only be constructed centuries later.

How was this possible? Was he a time traveler? How could one man possess such vast knowledge? Was he simply a man of extraordinary intelligence and boundless imagination, or did he receive guidance from higher entities? Leonardo's parents were not married, and because of this, he could not attend the Neoplatonic Academy. Instead, he spent much of his time in the Apennine Mountains studying the mysteries of nature. In his diaries, he describes a strange cave he discovered in the Apennines. Although he did not specify its exact location, it must have been significant enough to record in his writings. What did that cave represent to Leonardo? Was it there that he had his first encounter with extraterrestrials? Or did the cave conceal a portal or stargate that allowed him to travel into the future?

Between 1476 and 1478, there is a gap in his life. Leonardo virtually disappears from historical records, and there is no information about where he was or what he was doing during this period. Yet, it is precisely after this gap that his importance begins to emerge. So, where was he during those two years? Was he abducted by aliens and taken aboard their spacecraft, where he was instructed to bring significant progress to human civilization during its greatest enlightenment? This hypothesis echoes the biblical Enoch, who was taken by angels and taught divine mysteries and priestly rituals.

Leonardo himself provides clues that may answer these questions. As a young man, he apprenticed with Andrea del Verrocchio, one of the most renowned artists of the time. The most notable work of the Da Vinci-Verrocchio collaboration is undoubtedly The Annunciation, depicting the angel Gabriel announcing to the Virgin Mary that she would soon bear the Son of God. Verrocchio began the painting using tempera on an egg-based medium with lead-based colors, but Leonardo, strangely, used a different technique when painting the angel Gabriel. In a 1989 study, a detailed analysis confirmed that the angel was indeed painted by Leonardo. However, something very strange was discovered: when subjected to X-rays, the angel Gabriel became invisible because Leonardo used lead-free colors.

Why did Leonardo, the apprentice, use a technique different from his mentor's? Perhaps he wanted to leave a message. But what kind of message? Was he trying to tell us that, like the angel Gabriel, he was a divine or extraterrestrial messenger? That he traveled back and forth between our world and an alien world? Returning to the cave, why didn't he disclose its exact location? Many contactees report their first encounters occurring in the mountains, away from prying eyes. This was the case with Siragusa, Meyer, "Moses," and many others.

As you can see, there are many similarities between geniuses, prophets, and contactees. A prophet communicates with God, a contactee with aliens, while a genius who often receives enlightenment through visions, dreams, or images essentially experiences the same kind of connection. It is a single phenomenon with three different modes of communication. Why is a prophet who communicates with God widely accepted, while a contactee who communicates with aliens is not? Some might argue: "Well, we've never seen aliens, and there's no proof of their existence." But there is proof plenty of it! In fact, I would say there's more evidence for aliens than for God.

Let me clarify: I don't just believe in God I know God exists. The fact that so many people, across all ages, recount similar experiences is evidence in itself. And let's not forget the microchips or small implants found in the bodies of numerous abductees or contactees. But that's not the point. What I want to emphasize is that the role of the contactee has perhaps always been underestimated.

Leonardo spent a great deal of time in nature, which likely allowed him to reach an altered state of consciousness, enabling him to connect with the whole. Our pineal gland produces DMT during REM sleep at night. Rick Strassman, a psychiatrist, refers to DMT as the "spirit molecule," which serves as the biological basis for spiritual experiences, out-of-body experiences, and astral travel phenomena that often occur naturally in some individuals. Why does the human body produce a psychedelic substance that alters consciousness? Perhaps it's to enable us to connect with beings from other worlds. Could this be how Leonardo received his enlightenment?

And what if I told you there was another great genius in our history who openly declared that he had and utilized this ability? A name synonymous with genius itself: Albert Einstein. With his Theory of Relativity, he revolutionized physics and everything that was known at the time. Einstein would spend hours contemplating and seeking answers. Sitting in a chair, he meditated until he reached a deep state of trance. As he recounted, he could mentally travel to the very edges of the universe. He didn't receive answers; he observed them with his mind. When he formulated the Theory of Relativity, he described his mind as being struck by a storm.

I could give countless examples: all the great geniuses of history speak of dreams, visions, mental images, and unknown forces that somehow influence our reality. Isn't this the same thing contactees describe? How useful could the information received by contactees be for our science, technology, medicine, and so much more? I believe it is worth paying greater attention to these truly special individuals, who consistently demonstrate immense willingness to help others.

THE LIFE OF A CONTACTEE

Explaining the phenomenon of contactee experiences in scientific terms is a daunting task. Science lacks the tools to observe, study, and measure phenomena that transcend material reality. Reality is what we perceive with our five senses, but what would happen if we developed additional sensory abilities? With an expansion of our senses, our perception of what we consider reality would also broaden. Ten thousand years ago, humans could distinguish at most ten colors, whereas modern humans, thanks to the evolution of vision, can differentiate over three hundred. This illustrates that as humanity evolves, so does our perception of reality. We know that everything is energy; even matter itself is energy. Thus, as long as we think in terms of matter, we will never be able to comprehend what is not matter as we understand it. Nikola Tesla said, "If you want to understand the universe, think in terms of energy, frequency, and vibration."

If science cannot explain something, it does not mean that the phenomenon is not real. Thanks to the visionary minds of great geniuses throughout history who may themselves have been contactees (often labeled as insane) humanity has reached its current level of knowledge. What impact would full awareness of the existence of a universe beyond the physical have on an ordinary human being? How would it affect their daily life on psychological, ethical, and moral levels? This is an aspect of contactees that is rarely discussed, but I want to explore it here to highlight the difficulties these individuals face daily, battling indifference and prejudice from those who lack even the slightest awareness of certain realities.

The first thought that comes to a contactee's mind during an initial encounter with an alien reality is often that they have gone mad. In many cases, they withdraw into themselves, avoiding work or school, social outings with friends, and experiencing increased anxiety, depression, and general discomfort to the point of seeking help from a medical or psychological specialist. Rarely will they confide in anyone, not even a close friend or partner and who could blame them? Who would believe them? Only after a long period of adjustment does a contactee begin to understand their experience and their role. Aliens (the benevolent ones) are very careful not to cause trauma to the contactee, though even for them, initial encounters are not easy due to factors such as karma, soul contracts, mental conditioning, and external influences (negative aliens), among others.

Thus, the contactee receives only the information they need and only when they have fully processed and understood it can they move on to the next stage. After the initial disorientation and a long period of visions, resurfacing memories, strange phenomena (including paranormal events), and sightings of unidentified objects, a genuine collaboration begins between the contactee and the alien. This relationship often evolves into a deep bond of friendship or brotherhood.

Effectively, the contactee lives two parallel lives: one on Earth and another in a different dimension. The physical toll on these individuals is enormous. Living in the astral realm or in space requires tremendous energy, which takes a significant toll on the physical body, resulting in joint pain, backaches, severe migraines that can last for days, and even serious illnesses. For example, think of astronauts: prolonged stays in space can cause severe physical damage and illnesses due to radiation exposure.

But what does it mean to live in the astral? It means that humans are composed not only of a physical body but also of a spiritual body (spirit), a soul body (soul), and an astral body very similar to the physical body but made of much finer matter. Using the astral body, one can travel both within our world and into space. This may be difficult to understand or accept, but scientific studies (which I will delve into in the next chapter) and experiments demonstrate the existence of the astral body. Increasingly, scientists are embracing theories of the multiverse, parallel dimensions, and the existence of ethereal, non-material life forms.

As you may have realized, a contactee's life is extraordinarily demanding. But what happens during these encounters? Initially, the contactee is taught the secrets of the universe, their origins, and the history of our world and extraterrestrial civilizations. Once they reach a sufficiently high level of awareness, the contactee begins their mission, which includes spreading extraterrestrial messages and raising awareness about human rights, world hunger, climate change, environmental conservation, and nuclear disarmament. Additionally, they sometimes participate in military-style missions involving clashes between alien factions. Benevolent aliens hunt down negative ones the so-called Rebels.

From the information shared by contactees, I have learned of the existence of several alien bases on Earth, connected by underground tunnels, where collaborations between aliens and humans take place. There are also alien bases in deep oceans, lakes, mountain interiors, and Antarctica. According to contactee and abductee testimonies, horrifying events occur in these laboratories. Terrestrial and alien beings men, women, adults, and children are subjected to experiments, invasive medical examinations, torture, and various other abuses. All beings (terrestrial and extraterrestrial) are imprisoned, kept in cages or cylinders filled with strange liquids. The mission of the benevolent aliens is to free these imprisoned beings and capture the negative aliens, often with the help of contactees, who witness indescribable, inhumane scenes of cruelty.

Contactees, to avoid recognition, use their astral bodies inserted into cloned bodies. However, they too can be captured and subjected to the same abuses or even death. Although the astral body does not die, killing the cloned physical body allows them to experience death fully.

Imagine the trauma! Imagine the psychological frustration of it all. Living in war, enduring all the associated atrocities, and being in constant contact with absolute evil is no small feat.

Additionally, there is a more human aspect to consider: living daily life. It seems easy enough, but for a contactee, even the simplest things become significant challenges. Going to school, work, or simply hanging out with friends can be risky. Contactees are constantly watched: strangers approach them on buses or streets, asking embarrassing questions in the presence of friends or family, military personnel loiter in their neighborhoods, helicopters circle the area, homes are broken into, kidnapping attempts occur, and much more. This is all part of a contactee's daily life. In their presence, anything can happen: chandeliers explode, electricity goes out in entire buildings, appliances burn out, and streetlights turn off as they pass. How can they explain these phenomena to friends, family, or partners?

I remember once a dear contactee friend confided in me about how difficult it was for her to have a romantic relationship. She was stunningly beautiful, with a truly otherworldly charm and sweetness. She told me that one evening, while at home with her boyfriend, doors and windows began slamming on their own, and the electricity flickered. The two were in bed, and the boyfriend grew terrified. Although she knew the cause of the anomalies, she tried to reassure him, claiming it was the wind and that she had forgotten to close all the windows. After closing them, she returned to bed, but the sheets suddenly flew off without either of them touching them. The boyfriend fled and never returned. Today, this dear friend is in a happy relationship. She has not yet revealed everything about her alien activities, but she is taking it step by step so that her new boyfriend can acclimate to the reality. I'm confident he will accept her for who she is after all, love conquers all.

This is the life of a contactee: fighting a war that began at the dawn of time, known as the eternal struggle between Good and Evil, while simultaneously living a human existence amid ridicule and prejudice. Yet, despite everything, they are always ready to lend a helping hand to those in need. A contactee can always offer a word of comfort and transmit love and serenity to others. I cannot prove that everything contactees recount is real, but what if it is? Perhaps we should try to put ourselves in their shoes for once. Only then can we understand not only the uniqueness of their experiences but also their immense strength, altruism, and generosity in sharing their knowledge, often at great personal risk and peril.

INTERVIEW WITH DR. RAFFAELE RENNA

The world of contactism, despite various studies, remains a true mystery. In approximately eighty years of studies and research, no absolute truth has been reached yet, and perhaps it will take much more time for our civilization to reach a level of awareness capable of understanding the reality of existence not only of extraterrestrials but also of all the creatures of the universe and the universe itself.

Nowadays, we are still navigating a sea of theories, but we have one certainty: the phenomenon is real. People from all over the world, distant from each other in terms of geographical location, age, and culture, and belonging to different eras, all report the same experiences. The descriptions of "aliens," the sensations and emotions felt during these strange encounters, and even the descriptions of objects spaceships, their control panels, machinery used for clinical examinations, blood sampling, or surgical operations, beds with a single central leg, and much more are all described in exactly the same way, down to the smallest details.

Beyond the accounts, what gives greater credibility to the phenomenon is also the change observed in contactees, abductees, and those contacted after the encounter. These individuals have demonstrated an expansion of their higher self, also developing extrasensory abilities: clairvoyance, remote viewing, telepathy, premonition, and so on. For this reason, I wanted to ask the opinion of an expert, and I turned to someone who I consider, today, the most suitable person in Italy to address the issue: Dr. Raffaele Renna. Graduated in Educational Sciences with a psychological focus and later specialized in psychology, he is a researcher, lecturer, and author of dozens of articles and three books. Renna also has a YouTube channel followed by thousands of subscribers, where he shares his research, which I highly recommend following. Below, I report the questions asked to Dr. Raffaele Renna, whom I thank for his friendly participation.

What are the common characteristics among contactees? Before answering this question, it is necessary to make a distinction between a "contactee" and a "contacted person." The latter case assumes an alien abduction by unknown entities, which occurs when the victim undergoes an unusual (if not outright traumatic) and unplanned experience. Thus, the entities interact both with the body and the mind. A physical abduction may occur with the individual being transferred, against their will, onto (evidently super-technological) crafts, where they undergo surgical interventions on their bodies with more or less invasive and equally mysterious machinery. The motive behind such interactions is officially unknown and is entrusted to the expertise of psycho-analysts in such cases.

A contacted person, therefore, is not necessarily a contactee, while the latter is necessarily a contacted person. The visit made by a contactee aboard an unidentified object is referred to as a "ride," which in English literally means "passage," "ride," or "tour." The contactee declares themselves to be a bearer of a message for humanity and, at times, even for themselves. Most often, the victim reports receiving reassurances, through telepathic messages, that nothing will happen to them and, at the same time, begins to feel a sort of deep psychophysical relaxation in an altered state of consciousness.

Generally, the contactee describes these beings as benevolent in nature, and my decades of psycho-assistential work confirm this description. While it is true that no contactee has ever provided demonstrable evidence of their alleged encounters with alien life forms, on the other hand, telepathic revelations from these entities about facts, experiences, and premonitory events are often revealed through the work of psychologists and hypnotists (like myself), lending a certain credibility. Some of my clients, in this regard, have revealed to me manifestations of clairvoyance and an expansion of the Self capable of even preventing negative events.

How does that type of experience affect the life of a contactee? In practice, after providing the essential elements of the abduction phenomenon in the previous answer, all alleged abductees turn out to be, in some way, contactees, since the character traits and life changes that occur after that type of experience are very similar. This is, after all, the conclusion I have reached from assisting hundreds of contacted individuals.

It seems, with evidence in hand, that the interaction itself, by its very nature, constitutes a way to become a contactee. This often happens through word of mouth with trusted friends and family or by having the courage to spread to the wider world the more or less implicit message contained in the life change experienced by the individuals.

After an initial and understandable psychological attitude of bewilderment and dismay, the presumed contactee, even more than the contacted person, feels the need to communicate with humanity, perceives a change in their worldview, develops a capacity for self-criticism, but above all has a pronounced desire to be approved and gratified, initially struggling to manage their emotions. They feel detached from the rest of the world, even from their own family, and still have the sensation of coming from another planet (which they often dream about).

What impact does this type of experience have on family and friends? Unfortunately, in most of the cases I have dealt with (and also documented in the literature), the impact is negative due to the existential and ideological inadequacy that arises. The individual may sometimes feel compelled to separate from their partner and seek a new way of life and approach to others and the world.

Does the contactee have different brain functions than a "normal" person? No, they have simply undergone a sort of "brainwashing" and consequent resetting of their cognitive functions.

Have you ever noticed scientific, mathematical, astronomical, historical, or other knowledge in a contactee that they apparently could not have possessed? No, as already mentioned, they improve their performance and some abilities that they previously only had in potential. However, this does not exclude that many geniuses, artists, musicians, and scientists who have literally changed our world may be the result of the experimentation mentioned earlier, with the supposed genetic hybridization theorized by modern ufology (and also by myself).

Have you noticed improvements after such experiences, such as in reasoning, reflection, or learning? "Those who have interacted with aliens develop extraordinary abilities," revealed former U.S. spy Luis Elizondo. This confirms what I state in my two dossiers on abductions. Those who have had close encounters with these entities are forever changed... but for the better, developing previously unsuspected abilities.

Readers of my channel know that I have created two video dossiers on alleged abductions[1] (presented by Nick Pope). In these videos, I particularly highlight the psychological and character traits common to all these alleged abductees.

Is contact possible for anyone?

I don't believe in the culture of contactism or in the literature that emerges from it. Often, a contactee creates their character by writing books about what happened to them. And so far, I see no objection to this. However, when they found movements, even religious ones, declaring

____

[1] https://www.youtube.com/watch?v=rSQ2jX7-67w

themselves some sort of ambassador of extraterrestrials and spokesperson for their messages to the world, my interest in these so-called contactees diminishes. Surely they may have had extraordinary experiences, but by declaring themselves chosen or selected, they undermine what might be considered the true objective of these Lords of Space (as C. G. Jung called them).

These Lords of other worlds have no need to select suitable individuals for their purposes, as they have already been working on humanity's evolution for millennia, interacting in the ways previously described. Their work is laborious, and it may seem covert or obscure, but that is precisely what they are doing. A U.S. study in the 1990s estimated that at least 10% of humanity had been contacted or "genetically touched" by these beings. Often, the subject undergoes the interaction without recalling anything: they move on from it just as they do with many other events or episodes that our rational mind removes as a defense mechanism. Therefore, it is reasonable to suppose that, in 30 years, that percentage has at least doubled.

What is your opinion about this type of experience?

These entities exist (and saying this is hardly a revelation); they have always existed, and it should not be surprising that they have interacted with our planet and humanity for millennia. What remains to be discovered are the purposes of these interactions and the ultimate goals of this hypothetical experimentation. I have already made several videos on this topic, where I clarify what I have gathered from my clients: we are the result of their experimentation, which would easily explain the famous missing link in our evolution the quantum leap from ape to Homo sapiens.

Ultimately, all the contacted individuals are "contactees" relative to their personal experiences.

Considering what has been said so far, I do not know how much personal or economic success, for example, famous contactees like Claude Vorilhon (self-proclaimed last messiah or prophet and founder of the Raelian Movement), George Adamski, Billy Meier, Carlos Diaz, Howard Menger, Fernando Sesma Manzano (protagonist of a supposed contact with the Ummites), Elizabeth Klarer, Orfeo Angelucci, Riley Martin, or even Eugenio Siragusa (who deserves a separate discussion), actually gain. But I am convinced that what drives them to establish themselves and build their identities as messengers of these entities is the unconscious force of those mental archetypes that we all carry within us.

These forces, which we usually do not listen to or listen to poorly can lead us to become narcissistic, desiring recognition in the social sphere at all costs, whether for better or worse.

Is it possible that a connection, a sort of entanglement, has been created between the alien and the contactee?

We are all entangled, according to quantum theory. However, I have observed, through various accounts from my female clients of childbearing age who experienced such events, sometimes in traumatic ways, a strange subsequent emotional attachment to the event itself. Occasionally, this manifests as a rare but profound emotional connection or even a form of infatuation with an entity.

Will future generations be more predisposed to this type of experience?

At this point, I believe future generations (not very far away) will finally be up to the ethical and existential challenge, uniting with these entities and inaugurating a grand galactic celebration.

Are contactees more evolved people?

We need to agree on what we mean by the adjective "evolved." No, contactees-contacted individuals are not more evolved than others, but they are further along in understanding the world and themselves. They have a more expanded Self, with abilities they already potentially possessed but which have grown through the extraordinary experience, particularly in the artistic field. Surely, their performance in their work or profession improves, leading to better self-esteem and control of their actions.

How do you evaluate this type of experience, positive or negative?

Based on what has been said, I can only think of a gradual societal change for the better, a renewal of consciousness with new generations, and everything that may follow, viewed optimistically.

Jacques Vallée, the famous ufologist, stated that "no serious investigator has ever cared about the claims of contactees":

well, evidently, he hasn't seen or read my videos and articles on the subject.

DO MIRACLES EXIST?

Our personality, our thoughts, our emotions, our feelings, and our memories are closely tied to brain activity, yet somehow, they are also independent and more powerful than the mind itself, to the extent that they can survive death. Scientifically, it has been observed that individuals with flat electroencephalograms and electrocardiograms, declared clinically dead, were not actually dead. Thousands of such experiences tell us that there are many people who can recount everything that happened to them during resuscitation, down to the smallest details.

These individuals describe seeing themselves outside their bodies and finding themselves in a dimension where space and time do not exist. The individual does not identify with their body (although they know that body belongs to them) but rather with the entirety of existence. In hundreds of experiments, individuals who returned to life were able to describe not only the entire resuscitation process but also symbols, drawings, and objects intentionally placed two meters above ground level. Furthermore, they were able to accurately recount dialogues between the doctor and their family members.

All those who have experienced such an event claim to have encountered, in addition to relatives and friends, luminous beings often associated with angels, spiritual masters, deities, or aliens. One could thus affirm that life exists in an etheric, immaterial form. This form of life persists in other dimensions, imperceptible to our senses. This is not just speculation but a fact supported by scientific evidence.

I want to share the testimony of a dear friend and fellow townsman: the well-known entrepreneur from Atripalda, Stasio Della Porta, owner of the Atelier Sposa e Sposo Silvana Bruno.

"In 2017, I began to feel pain in my legs and back, but I didn't worry too much, thinking it was just the effects of aging. Over time, the pain intensified to the point that I was forced to go to the hospital. After undergoing the necessary exams, I was advised to be hospitalized. After a week of being admitted, I was told I needed urgent surgery, as the tumor mass had to be removed as soon as possible. The night before the surgery, I dreamed of a beautiful woman holding a child in her arms who smiled at me a figure remarkably similar to the Madonna of Montevergine. Upon waking up the next morning, I still remember feeling a strong sense of peace, despite knowing I would soon undergo a difficult operation.

Before the surgery, they performed new X-rays, which, incredibly, showed a completely different result: the tumor mass had disappeared entirely. After 30 days of hospitalization, the department head told me upon my discharge: 'I don't know what happened, but I'm certain you have a saint in heaven who truly loves you.' I, too, believe there was divine intervention. My relationship with faith has always been extraordinary, from a very young age. The miracle didn't change me. Believing does not mean being rewarded for a need; faith is not a give-and-take."

Similar stories come from every corner of the world: inexplicable healings, genuine miracles, are documented in all cultures worldwide. Even though science has no explanation, it is undeniable that miracles exist.

But how do miracles happen? And why not to everyone? As mentioned, those who experience miracles often recount encounters with luminous beings who tell them to go back because their time has not yet come. Who are these luminous beings? In ufology, there is extensive literature about immaterial entities called beings of light, who are said to live in equally immaterial worlds. According to contactees, the true form of existence is energetic or etheric a notion that reflects a spiritual vision and aligns with discoveries in quantum physics.

Thus, miracles may occur thanks to the intervention of aliens living in a state of existence different from ours. These beings are what we consider deities, angels, saints, and so on (in my opinion, even Jesus belongs to this higher level of existence).

But then, does only someone with faith or contact with beings of light experience miracles? Not exactly. First of all, it is the soul that decides its experience, whether in this or other dimensions. Each time the soul incarnates, it establishes the duration of its experience in other words, it decides when to die. According to the Universal Law of Free Will, no one can interfere unless it is truly necessary. For instance, if a soul destined to die at fifty years of age suffers a fatal accident, it will be brought back to life. The same applies to severe illnesses, as we saw with my friend Stasio. So, if it is not your time, nothing can end your life.

When an individual finds themselves in another dimension, the soul recalls its soul contract. If it still has lessons to learn or a mission to complete, it will return. Upon waking, the person will only have a vague memory of the place and the entities they encountered who helped them return.

But there are important points to consider. Some souls choose to experience illness and, for this reason, are not healed or do not self-heal (yes, because the soul can also do that). In such cases, there will be no miracle. At other times, serious illnesses or accidents are deliberately induced by negative entities that do not want the soul to complete its mission. In such cases, miracles occur.

Thus, in some cases, the person who experiences a miracle can be considered a contactee. This means they could one day become a full-fledged contactee.

Some may be upset, as they do not consider miracles something to be associated with aliens. Or there may be those who ask: if deities, angels, or Jesus are actually alien beings from another level of existence, does that mean God does not exist? Is believing in divinity wrong? Absolutely not. If everything is energy, life itself originates in energy. If God is the all-in-one and the one-in-all, it simply means that everything comes from God; everything is God itself. Nothing is created from nothing there must necessarily be a Creator behind all creation.

Therefore, even the most evolved beings in all creation are children of God. We are all souls created by a divine intelligence, and if we think about it, we are all aliens beings who do not originate from this world but from a Source-God, somewhere far away in the infinite universe.

I wanted to discuss miracles simply because they demonstrate, with scientific evidence, the existence of other dimensions and other forms of life, which we simplistically call alien. Understanding the world of contactees also means becoming aware of a reality different from ours, and just like a contactee, a person who experiences a miracle has come into contact with that reality.

I believe that miracle stories should also be explored to better understand our true nature and that of aliens. If, in the past, contact with entities from other dimensions was interpreted as divine, it is because people lacked the tools to understand it. This does not in any way cast doubt on faith in God or His existence.

I believe every being in the universe is a child of God and, as such, is themselves a deity, more or less aware of it. I think the person who experiences a miracle has had contact with another reality, and I believe that if they were given another chance, it is for a higher purpose.

As a ufologist and in intellectual honesty, I cannot deny the correlation between the experiences of contactees and those who experience miracles. Furthermore, in some cases of abductions, miracles have occurred: women who were unable to have children managed to successfully carry a pregnancy, or severe illnesses completely disappeared.

Of course, in these cases, the miracles were performed by negative entities, with the sole purpose of keeping the abductee alive because they serve their dark purposes. As mentioned, benevolent entities respect free will. Therefore, I encourage further research in this direction; if we want to achieve true knowledge, we must not neglect anything. Even a single piece can be essential to building the entire puzzle.

MESSAGES FROM ORION

In 2018, during a meeting of CUFOM (Mediterranean Ufological Center), besides the various members, a young female contactee was also invited. I remember being immediately struck by her story. While she spoke, I entered a sort of trance, and my mind was transported to the times of ancient Egypt. Images of hieroglyphs, pharaohs, pyramids, and supernatural beings alternated in my mind. I had read the Emerald Tablets of the God Thoth, and that girl gave me the impression that, in some way, she belonged to that era and I wasn't mistaken.

Laurienit (this is the name she was given by the extraterrestrials) recounted having contacts with the Neteru of the Orion Belt, who revealed to her the secrets of humanity's origins and the alien presence in our world, a presence that has endured since the dawn of time.

From that day on, we often stayed in touch, and a beautiful friendship was born. She is a sweet girl and has a way of communicating that goes straight to the heart. Her encounters with aliens began at a very young age, but only after turning eighteen did her awakening journey start. Today, she is fully aware of the alien reality and her role.

Laurienit lives her relationship with the aliens (or, as she prefers to call them, "her people") with absolute freedom; she could end it at any moment, but she has chosen to collaborate and contribute, though not without difficulties. As we have seen, living between two realities is far from easy. Moreover, Laurienit actively participates in the dissemination of the alien phenomenon, not only in Italy but also abroad, often at her own expense.

Before sharing the channeled message from Laurienit for all of us, I will briefly explain who the Neteru are and why they are so important.

In a very distant time, beings from another universe attempted to attack the Orion Nebula to steal its vital energy. A terrifying war broke out, remembered today as a metaphor in cultures worldwide: the battle between Good and Evil, Lucifer's Rebellion, Light versus Darkness, and so on. The people of Orion, with the help of other star nations, managed to repel the Rebels, but it was decided to create a new race capable of protecting the Nebula and ensuring balance across the universe.

From the Nebula, divine intelligence created a new mixture by combining genetic material from multiple races with new substances, essences, and energies, unique in its kind, and merged it with the life essence of the people of Alnilam, the central star of the Orion Belt. This is how the Neteru were born: beings of infinite love, connected to the natural cycle of the universe. Their mission is to protect the Nebula, all the stars, planets, and dimensional portals of our universe.

The Neteru are considered the Guardians of the Galaxy and lead the Galactic Confederation, an association of multiple peoples united in the battle against the Rebels. Their presence is mentioned in many ancient texts: the Book of Enoch speaks of divine beings called Watchers, the Bible refers to the Nephilim a term often translated as giants, though its root derives from Nephilah, meaning Orion. In the Americas, the Hopi called the Neteru Katchinas, or star beings.

The three Hopi Mesas perfectly represent the Orion Belt, while their other villages symbolize the entire constellation. Other constructions connected to Orion are found in Mexico, Peru, Hawaii, China, Polynesia, and many other locations worldwide. However, the Neteru are most closely associated with ancient Egypt.

About 40,000 years ago, a global frequency drop occurred, exacerbated by interference from Rebel races. As the ancient Hindu Vedic texts recount, during that time, thousands of alien races interacted with our world, maintaining relationships with human rulers. It was the age of great Atlantis, an era marked by corruption, greed for power, and evil spread across the planet, oppressing innocent people. For this reason, the Neteru decided to intervene.

With the arrival of the Neteru, one cycle ended, and a new one began. The great flood swept away all corrupt nations, including Atlantis. The Atlantean Thoth was tasked by the Neteru to save righteous humans with specific skills. Thus, the Neteru left Atlantis and settled in the land of barbarians: ancient Khem, known today as Egypt.

The Neteru initiated Egyptian civilization and built the pyramids, where they concealed ancient knowledge. The pyramids served a protective function, maintaining a specific frequency across the land. They also built other pyramids in different parts of the world, always with the same purpose. After about 16,000 years, the Neteru left Egypt, succeeded by the Shemsu Hor, semi-divine beings tasked with instructing the new rulers.

This was the First Time, or Zep Tepi, according to the historian-priest Manetho. A similar story is told in Sumerian texts, referencing a specific post-diluvian period when the Apkallu, seven wise semi-divine beings, taught humanity how to rule.

The Orion Nebula was known in ancient Egypt as the god Ra, the creator of worlds, demonstrating the advanced knowledge of the Egyptians. Today, it has been discovered that the Orion Nebula, or M42, is indeed central to the creation of our universe. Everything in our universe originated from the Nebula-Ra, but how could the ancient Egyptians have known this? It's obvious! They were instructed by the Neteru.

So, can we say that the Nebula-Ra is God? The answer is no. Imagine the universe as a gigantic body: the Nebula is just one of the many organs that compose it. Ra is not God but one of the many Spirits that serve the functioning of the entire body. In this case, Ra would represent feminine energy the womb. Other Nebulae would represent other organs. The whole body is God.

After this brief summary, I want to share with you the message from Orion, channeled by Laurienit.

Orion:

"You are not alone and have never been alone. We all come from the same Source-God; you are no less than any being in the universe. You are divine souls and have everything you need to grow. The time has come to choose. The path to your personal growth is clear and right in front of you. You may stay where you are or turn back, but know that this will bring you suffering.

Do not let yourselves be conditioned by religious dogmas or the current system that seeks to keep you asleep, trapped in companies producing things that, for over 90%, you will not need at all. Work is important, and everyone must contribute to the well-being of society. But do not let it become a trap. Produce only what you need, and dedicate more time to educating your children.

Do not be afraid: if you are here and involved in certain dynamics, it is because your soul is no longer in vibration with this society. When the frequency drops, connection to the whole is lost, and duality, detachment, and pain are felt. There is no more time: have the courage to leap into the fourth dimension. Only you can do it do not wait for false prophets. This time, no one will do it for you.

How to do it?

Orion:

Work on yourselves. Clear away the past that still torments you. Let go of the past, practice forgiveness. Rediscover the value of family, friends, nature, and the whole. Talk to yourselves; your soul will respond. Remember, it knows everything. Practice; ask, and you will receive answers.

Regain your inner peace, love yourselves, love life, and you will reconnect with the whole. You have the ability and all the means to do so. You are not alone and have never been alone.".

ACKNOWLEDGMENTS

We wish to express our profound gratitude to those who made the realization of this project possible.

A heartfelt thank you goes to Dr. Raffaele Renna, whose expertise and passion for research have significantly enriched the content of this book. His dedication to the analysis and understanding of cosmic phenomena has been a constant source of inspiration.

A special thanks also to Stasio Della Porta, a witness to extraordinary events, whose support and encouragement have had a fundamental impact on our journey. His vision and critical approach have stimulated valuable reflections, contributing to shaping the message we wish to convey.

Finally, our gratitude to Laurienit for her invaluable contribution and her willingness to share ideas and insights by channeling the message expressed in this writing. All this has made this journey even more stimulating.

We also extend our thanks to Prof. Ermelinda Calabria for her continuous and irreplaceable support, without which the drafting of this small essay would not have been possible.

To all of you, our sincerest recognition. Thank you for believing in this project and for supporting me along the way.

Giuseppe Corcione & Giovanni Pellegrino

www.ingramcontent.com/pod-product-compliance
Lightning Source LLC
Chambersburg PA
CBHW051758250726
48659CB00001B/492